Gilded Hours

Poems from the Williamsburg Poetry Guild

Editor: Ann Marie Boyden

Associate Editors: Ron Landa
E.S. von Gehren
Wheston Chancellor Grove

Copyright © 2013 by The Williamsburg Poetry Guild

ISBN 978-0-7414-9604-1

Printed in the United States of America

Published August 2013

INFINITY PUBLISHING
1094 New DeHaven Street, Suite 100
West Conshohocken, PA 19428-2713
Toll-free (877) BUY BOOK
Local Phone (610) 941-9999
Fax (610) 941-9959
Info@buybooksontheweb.com
www.buybooksontheweb.com

In memory of
Andrea Rawson

The soul of the
Williamsburg Poetry Guild
is an amalgam of all we call,
or have called, "member".
This is especially true of
those who have
departed this life,
for it is by their
writings that we
still know them.

TABLE OF CONTENTS

*Williamsburg Poetry Guild President Flora Bolling Adams
and Friend on Duke of Gloucester Street, Williamsburg.*

PREFACE

This small volume showcases but a sampling of the works created by members of the Williamsburg Poetry Guild (the Guild). In style, voice, theme - in all dimensions of poetic discourse - these works reflect the diversity that is found in the lives of the Guild members. As you go through this volume, sampling the different poets, you will journey through a rich fabric of world environments (far western plains, seascapes...), emotional struggles/joys, places in space and time, enjoyment of events, or just outright whimsy. It is all here, just as our members have opened themselves, their lives, their aspirations, their memories, for all to experience with them.

As is true of Williamsburg in general, few of the members are native to this area, but all share the common bond of the written word, as it sings to their need for personal expression. As a formal entity the Williamsburg Poetry Guild got its start in 1997 as an outgrowth of a poetry class given by our first president Rita Durrant. Over time, like minded poets have been invited to membership, always with the thought of maintaining a small but talented group. The poetic life has been characterized as a solitary existence, and so it would be without the camaraderie of the mutual sharing among members, the opportunities to share with eager listening groups among the public, and the occasional publication such as this anthology represents. The greatest tribute a poet can receive is to be appreciated by others. With this said, we wish that you the reader will enjoy our words and appreciate the world of our poetry.

As poets are wont to do we couldn't resist the voiced ambiguities in the title we've given this anthology - *Gilded Hours*. Though the urge is great to explain, we must leave it to you, the reader, to play with the title and make of it as you wish.

Sunrise

ANDREA CHRISTENSEN RAWSON

Raised in South Carolina, Andrea was a renaissance woman. Hospice, YMCA, an arts council for the eastern shore community, Onancock, where she lived before coming to Williamsburg. Boats and rivers, church and home, mother of six, PTA, teaching, speaking, and of course writing poetry. Her poems are strong and wise, sometimes autobiographical, often with a point-of-view. Whether she was reciting *Prologue to Canterbury Tales* or sharing her own work at the Poetry Society of Virginia reading, she did so with contagious enthusiasm and surprising vigor. Always supportive, she encouraged her fellow poets to do their very best. She is missed.

AIN'T NOTHIN' CHANGE'

"Glad you come by; coffee pot on de stove;
sit on de porch; see my pretty crape myrtle.
Min' what I sayin' to you: ain't nothin' change'."

"Grandma, why are you saying that?
Don't I have a college degree;
I'm the principal of Mossy Oaks Elementary:
and your grandson, an environmental engineer,
works for the government in Washington, D.C.
We have come a long way from when you
earned $4 a week cooking in white folks' kitchens."

"When I growin' up our church and neighbor
help raise children. Daddies no good, lef' home
or fathers work hard but not makin' it.
We hang close; we manage; we look after.
Today ain' nobody aroun'; chillren, dey jus' roamin'.
Y'all gettin' so far up, you don' see ones lef' behind.
Dose dat move on don' look back."

"We have a black President, Grandma,
the most powerful man in the whole world
and he is black!
Doesn't that tell you something BIG has happened!"

"O we proud of dat? Even white folks
think dey done somethin' good,
something moral; take away all dat bad,
but look how dey treat him, disrespect him!
Nobody say 'Shame! Shut yo' mouth!'
Won' let dey children listen to their President
tell dem study, stay in school, be good.
Why? 'Cause deep down dey still thinkin'
he jes a black boy actin' up."

2

Honeysuckle Summer

three skinny, adolescent cousins, triplets
with peeling sunburned noses,
sewed dirndl skirts
out of two yards of flowered seersucker.

strung together
carefully gleaned beach-shell necklaces
ensembles to beguile
the soda jerk at Luther's drugstore,
current community heart-throb.

along dusty roadsides
honeysuckle tangles gave off
sultry perfumes.

a mystic ritual,
sipping nectar from a flower
invested with magic powers,

we three novices
would know
romantic fantasies realized.

are you the answer
that golden nectar promised?

hey, sweet man,
you really took your time.

THE SNOWFLAKES

THERE IS A PERFECTION
WE CAN NEITHER PERCEIVE NOR ALTER,
SO EPHEMERAL, IMPRACTICAL, ABSURD
IN ITS ORIGINALITY, PROFUSION, PRODIGALITY
HUMAN ARROGANCE CAN NEITHER TRANSCEND NOR CORRUPT.

EACH DESIGN, UNIQUE, EXQUISITE, DISSOLVING,
AN ALTERNATE UNIVERSE PERHAPS
BEYOND ALL HUMAN RECKONING, THEORIES, EQUATIONS,
A MIRACLE, A WARNING, UNHEEDED, UNVALUED.

WHAT IS GOD TRYING TO TELL US
ON THIS CRYSTALLINE
CHRISTMAS MORN?

VOYAGES

The motor coughed and caught,
black sky still sparkling
with stars,
bay brilliant and beckoning
as we started across before dawn.

We passed Thimble Shoals
before noon
entering the great harbor
of Hampton Roads.

Dwarfed by tankers, skyscrapers, carriers,
ducked under five drawbridges
on the Elizabeth River,
leaving those snooty sailboats behind,
and waited at the locks at Great Bridge.

By afternoon I watched the
markers closely,
as we crept across Currituck Sound,
its shallow waters unforgiving
of any deviation from the
narrow channel.

At sunset we anchored behind
golden marshes
atwitter with red-winged blackbirds
on Blackwater Creek.
I boiled shrimp, letting the
shells drop over the fan tail.

Later you made up our bunk;
we rocked all night to the gentle
sound of water lapping,
our dreams startled by the
cry of the great blue heron
disappearing
into a bank of fog at daybreak.

Final as your departure, O my love!
I am set adrift on uncharted waters.

XMAS '06

HEY SANTA BABY,
I WANT A BRAND NEW HEART ---
NO BROKEN PARTS.
HOW ABOUT A HIP THAT SWINGS,
A VOICE THAT SINGS JOY TO THE WORLD,
JUST FOR A START.

LET'S ADD A FLEXIBLE KNEE
TO HANG FROM THE TREE,
EYES STAR BRIGHT,
TEETH THAT ARE WHITE,
FAULTLESS MEMORY.

FORGET ALL THE ABOVE
FOR A WORLD FILLED WITH LOVE,
A GOD'S-EYE VIEW
MAKING ALL THINGS NEW.
YOU CAN DO IT, TOO.
YES, YOU CAN!

SANTA BABY, YOU'RE THE MAN!!!

Dogwoods

FLORA BOLLING ADAMS

Flora is a native Virginian who has extended her love for teaching into retirement. She writes stories and poems for children and others who choose to stay young. She finds herself toying with the child's mind in the adult and believes that every piece of literature holds a special message waiting for its appropriate delivery. Her work appears in anthologies and in her own published books. She enjoys close association with other poets and follows Rita Durrant and Philomene Hood as the third President of the Williamsburg Poetry Guild. After her artist husband, Kelsey, passed, she moved from Williamsburg to Toano where Kirk and the three others bring her seven grandchildren and three greats for her to adore and try to feed a little poetry.

Powhatan's Lament

My tent is not folded, yet,
though my bones tire fast.
I have lost count of the moons,
but I feel that fewer than few are left for me.
The white man has come and now
lays waste over our nation,
pushing aside even the great Powhatan
from the wide waters of Chesapeake.
The Powhatan warriors beat their chests
at the sight of me;
the squaws from the Patuxent to
the south flowing waters
look on me with longing in their eyes.
Why then, do I feel powerless?

The pink-hairs with eyes like the sky
and the yellow-heads who wear buckles that gleam
look at our hardy squaws with disdain.
They eye our maidens with lust
and charm our young ones with whittled toys.
Why do they come in white-winged canoes
without women to start a new life?
They dangle baubles in front of
our keen-eyed brothers,
robbing our tribe of our ways and traditions.
They build walls around their settlements,
creating suspicion among my warriors.
How long can I contain them?
They give their own names to places.
Who is James that he should be so honored?

Every one of them wears heavy cloaks and
just as many need to wash in the cold water
that surrounds us. My senses of smell and sight
have become an abomination to me.
Tonight, after I have shared life
with my favorite squaw and I seek comfort
with my head on her arm,
I will listen for a sign to assure me that
the great tent above which stretches from horizon to horizon
will shelter, nurture, and strengthen me
and all the Powhatans for many squash times
and moons and moons and moons.

Sibling Love

They were five of a kind
like birds of a feather,
devoted to each other,
kept in close touch
with chords, cards, and calls.
The first flew away
from a month of grief and loneliness.
She kept love's promise to follow,
to come along soon.

And then there were four.
Bending the same branch, keeping
love alive.
The third flew away
from pain and disillusionment.
She lost the battle but won her peace.

Now, there are three
left huddled together
to miss their songs.
No tears can well to blur vision
of what the future will be:
Must the cameras flash this sad hour?
Loved ones want something to hold
and they are thinking: which
will be next to lie in the box?
Hard, on the outside,
Soft, on the inside.

Waltz of a Cloud

I am a cloud, a cumulus cloud
    Above the earth three/quarter time.
I'm tossed about away up high
    By currents strong in friendly sky.
The sun shines through and parts my wool,
    It lights my cold and sheepy mass,
It lines my edge with a silvery, silvery, silvery sheen.

I am a cloud, a cirrus cloud
    up in the cold ice-crystal sky.
My life is brief, depending on
    the drops of vapor waiting by,
And when I'm full and can't contain
    another speck of raindrops clear,
It is then that I cry, and I cry, and I cry and cry.

Oh, for a sweet and gentle rain
    down on the meadow lush and green;
Oh, for a warm and soaking drain
    out on the grove and pasture land;
My love will be charged with streaks of light
    exploding in the spacious sky,
Then thunder will crash and roll on out to the sea.

I was a lamb, a bleating lamb,
    Bouncing in pastures bountiful;
The sun went down, and darkness fell,
    I could not see the forms below.
I closed my eyes and eased my pain
    In wispy, delicate sheets of rain;
How could I know that my tears would chill to flakes of snow?

All the blooms under a blanket,
All perennials with cold feet,
Every tree a glass-covered skeleton
Bearing the snow and the sleet.
Oh, for a spring rain on the meadow,
Oh, for a dousing rain in the glen,
I shall insolate back to the heavens
And reign again, and rain again, and again.

Ripe Oranges
(After Reading Wallace Stevens)

Oranges are orange;
  not red or green or yellow
  like apples, but orange,
  not smooth, but bumpy,
  undulating rinds like knotted
  threads knit into knickers.

Oranges are round like balls;
  not odd-shaped like pears
  and bananas.
Thumbnail one at the stem scar;
  smell the sneezy zest,
  the peal of peel!
Taste the yippy juice,
  tangy, refreshing citrus
  like life new every second, but
  not like limes and lemons
  needing sugar to straighten a pucker.

Ripe oranges are orange,
  none varying.
  Orange you glad?

Little Cottonwood Canyon

ANN MARIE BOYDEN

I have been writing since I could hold a pencil.

At the University of Utah my diploma would have said *summa cum laude* if there had been WORD with spell check at the time.

For almost twenty-five years I wrote advertising for a living. Even won some awards. Somewhere in there, while still running the agency, I went back to school and earned a Master's Degree in Management and Business. Working in Washington I got to play with architects as Executive Director of the American Institute of Architects Trust. Mostly, the writing was technical, but hey!

Now I get to focus on poetry, some prose, cooking, golf, and photography.

August Cornfield

When we were young
we took beer into
an August cornfield.
Lying in fertile furrows,
sinking into Weber Valley,
we picked warm cobs
from the bottom of
towering stalks.
The smell of the silk
filling us with lust.
Shucking it,
feeding each other,
eating it raw,
washing it down
with warm beer
in the pristine
soil of Utah.
When we were young.

Emily Dickinson Museum

It isn't perfect - yet it's perfect –
Tangled snarled ancient beautiful –
August Roses bloom full
Anticipating chubby Daffodils –
Her little Sexton sings again –
Bees find flowers they prefer –
September Daylilies paint
Dashing strokes foretelling
Iris in May – on the lawn
Dandelion tales – Brawny Oak
Reaches for the sky as we
Find where it's been –
Ready to burst rusty buds
On giant Magnolias signal rebirth –
In the woods delicate Lady's Slippers
Or papery Trillium greet descendants
Of snakes and Poisonous plants
That led Emily to discover – not goblins –
Only angels –

> **Homage following a visit to**
> **Emily Dickinson's Garden**
> **where her words still live.**

Requiem in Common Time

One
The time you said to me
I'm proud of you,
the way you've lived your life.
I should have said,
"Do you believe in one way to be?"

You taught me algebra;
no one else could.
Is there a formula?
An equation?
An unintelligible peal scheme?

Then nine tailors,
and ninety-seven more.
I should have said,
"Thank you, I love you too."
Maybe I did.

Two
That time I died
I didn't see the light
or tunnel or winged being.
Gloria in excelsis.

A child of sound,
that time I died,
I heard The Mormon Tabernacle Choir.
a great featherbed of sound

multi-layered, big and soft.
Crescendo. Diminuendo.
Spongy and sheltered, in eight parts.
whooosh, plunk. hisssss, clunk -

or was it the ventilator?
That time I died
I didn't count three hundred voices,
there was one. Full forte.

Incapable of pianissimo.
I can never understand the words.
No one can.
D.C. Al fine.

That time I died, I didn't.

Three
Today they laid the grass down
smooth and dry on eighteen feet
of the valley floor by box elders
and Lucy's having been there.

Now the son of a treble shawm
lies silent. Sweet sound gone
wherever charmers go.
Serene Oboe d'amore.

Tomorrow they will lay
a Beta gentleman worthy of the name
in another place where an oboe
mourns.

Four
Emily says
it's a gentleman,
who kindly stops.

Wolfgang feared it,
and wrote a score for it.
So did Leonard.

The Harvard Guru says,
"One year is the same thing.'
Or is it a woman

carrying spring tulips,
and a beginning?
My very good friend says,

"I respect death.
it's the only thing that could
kill my Mother.
And all those
times I wanted to."

**Manga is the Japanese
word for comics.**
At least that's what we're told.

Manga
Japanese calligraphy
from 1798

They are real,
with perfect faces,
and huge, dark, blank eyes.
Androgynous ones
with mops of spiked hair

and ragged bangs.
With flowing scarves
and puffed-up jackets,
they are cross-dressers and flirts.
They are real,

consorting with rogue death gods.
Some possessed by animals
of the Chinese zodiac.
With long, long legs
they time-travel

to meet ghosts and devils.
Some with gigantic thighs
dwell in the past and
are just visiting here.
They are real.

Half-demons and soul-reapers,
finders of death notes.
They can be seen on the streets,
in the shops, in the schools.
They can be seen.

House above the Sea

RITA DURRANT

Rita earned her M.A. degree in Literature in 1980 at Governors State University. She authored the book, *College After 30*, in 1981 and taught at Holy Family College in Philadelphia. As a freelance writer, many of her articles and poetry were published in magazines and scholastic and literary journals. She served as a poetry instructor for the Christopher Wren Association at the College of William & Mary for six years. She was the first President of the Williamsburg Poetry Guild and editor of *Images of Williamsburg,* an anthology of poems written to honor the 300th anniversary of the city's founding. Her collection of poems, *Dancing to the Marigold Mazurka,* was published in 2010.

Joy and Sorrow

When your joy is eating at your table,
your sorrow is asleep in your bed.
                    Khalil Gibran

Trees flamed scarlet and gold
at the old Quaker Cemetery,
where a slight silver rain fell.

Ghosts rose up from November mists
as I sped toward the River Road.
Suddenly, a handsome pheasant appeared
his teal necklace, white circlet
and golden body gleaming.

Graceful tail feathers swept out
to brush the ground. Then he turned
his tiny crested head as if to question
my approach, alert to protect his family's nest.

I slowed my speed, delighting
in his bold stance, the orderly confusion
of gorgeous plumage. All kingliness
and majesty he was against
the frosted brown of earth,
the somber sculpture of stone fence.

Then as I began to pass, he panicked,
flung his body at my wheels...
and as I watched
in my rearview window,
tried to lift his slender neck,
struggled, then collapsed ...
and for a second,
my mind flashed back to another day,

my blue-eyed son,
who fell as I watched him from my window ...
and I wanted to take that still
soft creature in my arms,
caress him, beg him back,
but I could not.

The Singer Sewing Machine

I remember you, Mother,
working in the cold back parlor
at the black iron Singer
sewing machine, your raven hair
brushed back and caught in a bun
with tiny spit curls at your temples
like Dolores del Rio, movie star.

Your feet press back and forth
in rhythm on the treadle
as your hands guide the cloth
into the path of the bobbing needle,
the wheel whirring like an electric fan.

You are designing calico dresses
for beautiful Dorothy and me.
I, the painfully plain child,
with mouse-brown hair.
You are making frocks with fluffy skirts
puffed out like cotton candy,
and pinafores with tiny
smocked stitches, all the finery
you dreamed of wearing as a child.

You are bending over dainty costumes
for my ballet recitals,
fashioning golden wire wings
of gossamer silk, tulle tutus,
ruffles on stiff petticoats,
and satin ribbons for little waists.

And I remember…the first recital.
After all your tedious work,
I was the one ballerina
who did my own *"tour jette,"*
and *"petit bouree,"* pirouetting alone
while the other fairies danced together
as they were trained. But afterward,
you hugged me just the same,
and told me I danced like the Fairy Princess!

I'm still doing my own dance, Mama.

Wartime Wedding, 1945

We were too wise to fall in love, we said,
but we had one perfect sunny day
to spend, with royal palms
waving in wild tropical winds
along Miami's Biscayne Bay,
and the sky as lavender blue
as a Wedgewood bowl.

So we turned our backs on war.
He picked a red hibiscus for my hair
and we drove a rented Ford
to Lauderdale by-the-Sea
where we found a white-spired church.

At a small hotel by the shore
we spilled sparkling wine
on white linens, taking tiny sips
as if in sacramental rite,
toasting each other, our parents,
and the children we hoped to have one day.

Then we tasted our wedding feast
while night-blooming jasmine
sent gifts of heady fragrance up to us
from the garden below our balcony,
a giant pearl moon rolled around heaven,
and U-boats prowled off shore.

When I Am Old

When I am old, I will live on a hill
high above the sea,
and watch the waves
come thundering in
with the fury of a Bach fugue.

In winter, I'll light a hickory fire,
spin myself into a woolly cocoon,
and listen for the footsteps
of all my darling children
who wrapped up my heart
and stole it away.

When they come,
we'll take tea with lots of sugar,
dine on Peppermint Patties
and talk about important things;
like playmates, puppies, and grandpas,
and we'll listen to the sea play
a wild cantata in the icy wind.

In spring, I will drowse on my porch swing,
amid azalea blooms scarlet and pink,
delight in the purple violets,
the snowstorm of dogwood blossoms,
and the shimmering sea
will swell and sigh in the sun.

In summer, my children come once more;
we'll search for shells in the sand,
listen to songs of meadow larks,
and hear hummingbirds fluttering
at my feeder, beating the air.
We will hear songs of sea-sirens
luring lonely sailors out to sea.

Autumn will be late.
September will linger with skies
blue as a Dutchman's pants.
Leaves will turn harvest colors:
maize, pear, and persimmon.

The fragrance of smoky fires
will waft in the wind,
and sea monsters maraud
in the moonlight,
taking big bites of the shore.

And when I grow weary
of earthly beauty,
my Master will whisper,
"Arise, my beloved;
come with me,"
and I will.

The Backyard

JOANNE GOODE

I've never met a pizza I didn't like. My abs are almost
a six-pack. I meditate while power walking. I'm still
a Christian but I gave up church for Lent. I think teddy bears
have a secret life. At seventeen I was crushed when my teacher
said you don't have a dancer's body.
I spent my life trying to find myself in Colorado
but she's lost.

I could travel full-time with my husband in a seventeen-
foot camper if we follow good weather. Isn't it funny
that Georgia O'Keeffe was turned down flat
by the College of William & Mary as an art teacher?
I want to walk into the sunset next time I'm in New Mexico.
Without the sun I might as well shrivel up and die. If I were a dog
I'd be a golden retriever. I've hiked to fourteen-thousand feet
seven times in the past five years. When I die they better not
put me in the ground. I should have about thirty summers
left in me.

Once I held a hummingbird in my palm
tried to coax it back to life
then cried like the world was over
when it died.

The Mug

Did I tell you this mug belongs to me?
See, it says "mine MINE mine" here on its side, leaving
no shadow of doubt who the rightful
owner is declared to be (me). I could deign to let you
hold the handle, allow you to be the "mine" smiling
at me over its seafoam porcelain edge where the painted gulls
squeak and screech their ownership – can't you see –
they claim it for me, instead!
Mine mine MINE! I like the sound and tone –
a simple declaration carrying its own fame
a four-letter word (never profane)
rhymes nicely with sublime which is the feeling
I have as I wrap my fingers around
its sturdy coffee-filled frame
knowing I may have no other wealth to claim
except for this unique-made-in-Taiwan mug labeled mine
MINE mine.

And now, we're apart, you and me
I'm alone with my mug
I clasp its handle and remember the last time
we sat on a deserted beach
you reading Stephen King
and me scripting desperate poetry.
Today, I'm not thinking of aquamarine water
white crests of waves, cloud puffs
or footprint-rippled sand, sweet sunshine
but only how I wish you had held me tight
like a mug and told the world, she's mine
MINE mine.

Soliloquy for e

The silent e —
a doorstop at the end of my name
holding the *nn's* in place — a brick
that might stub your toe if you
weren't watching.
As appearances go, e makes *Joanne*
complete, full of purpose. Definitive.
And though she tries hard
not to offend
hanging there on the end
her soundless views are black and white.

This silent e —
keeps vigilance over my other letters
without her, they'd be leaning —
reckless, they might wander by accident.
e is a sturdy companion
dependable to a fault, no one ever
believes she's reserved and shy.

Time and again I have wished
for my e —
to be the soft, beautiful *a*
the kind of letter *J*
could wrap arms around.
Not afraid to play
stays in the moment, makes everyone
happy and never worries about
passing time.

Still, e surprises me with her
passionate, creative, sensitive side and
I might imagine my life-rungs
to be less hard to climb
        without e —
but after fifty-some
years as a collective one —
        without silent e
the other letters
would feel out of sorts
and quite forlorn.

Sweatin' it Out in Austin

Outside Patsy's Cowgirl Cafe, Austin traffic rushes by
while an Oklahoma-bred ranch boy plays guitar
I'm listenin' hard and we both let our dreams fly.

Way, way west of Nashville, another slow Tuesday night
it's empty tables, a few local folks at the bar –
he sings to my ears alone as the traffic slides by.

Cowboy hat, fresh face, boy-next-door honest eyes
fingers dancin' on strings – he's a real star –
sweatin' music deep from his pores, lettin' his dreams fly.

Me, I'm struck with inspiration – a wildfire ignites
I see notes of restless poetry smokin' cigars
and I'm graspin' at word-wisps. Traffic blows by.

At the break he comes over with an easy country smile
you've got talent, I say, you could take it so far
he thanks me kindly, says, it's family makin' my dreams fly.

Another Tuesday evenin', is he playing Patsy's tonight?
I'm home, sweatin' my own prose – notes flat and charred.
Still, like him, I can't give in to traffic's ceaseless cry –
so I rhyme, dream, believe. And sometimes, sometimes, I fly.

say this

say i decide i can't take this squirrel cage world. let me off i say
i don't care if i get dizzy standing on natural ground. say i transport

myself to a desert in new mexico and i walk into a flaming sunset
without a thought of tomorrow without thoughts of my nanny job

oiling the cogs of the career-wheels our profit-driven society
is driving. say i talk to my teddy bear and he responds in kind

telling me i'm not crazy to want a simple stressless life. take me
with you he cries. say I leave him sitting on the bed for my

granddaughter to find. she needs him more than i. say in twenty
years she meets me on a college break in california we share a sunset

wishing to god we knew one another better, that there was a world
we should have explored when she was three. instead.

say i realize
today is the only day we have.

say it again.
and again.
again.

Windlust

WHESTON CHANCELLOR GROVE

(1984-?) is an anachronism. Born and raised in Northern California just before the cusp of electronic mania and internet communication, he moved to the East coast at 13. He has been writing since he was 11 years old. He paints when passion compels him. He loves the mountains and his bilingual dachshund, "Kleine Baum" Tuck.

Wheston is at odds with the contemporary world and longs for a quieter place and time. "All charm and grace have been lost to a bygone era. And with it the woman of my dreams," says he. *Ashened Rapture,* a compendium of poetry, prose, short stories, and photographs, was published in 2011.

The Yellow Sky
(The Edge of the Earth)

My but
don't these words all blend—
All the things I've said and done—
Have I seen these things or were they in me?
Is it what I heard or what I knew?
The sky was yellow, the storm
a close welcome, jaundiced—

Down I lie—a wandering hand that came
to rest, relishing the prelude—a still body
and window's view—a slipping sky.
One lasting glow—passage for the
pure infected, prostrated bellows
sealing up the narrow path, fast drooping.
A slow, gentle rain, a shudder of the
walls—a single strand of lightning—
limbs tremble beneath the brow of foliage—the pale
hue wans—a brooding sky—calm
in its wistful gale—

Four yellow walls—the light zipped up—
a silver strand—Halved, each hemisphere
conveys, the atmosphere compresses,
doors of vision closed—
Day's view becoming night,
the pall of waking—
Its being—given in pantomime exchange—
the sallow yoke without
enters me—
Parasite or sacrifice?—
I give it life—
The host of its cause—
burden or companion?—

I took the world inside, swallowed it by piece—ill with
fathomless charge,
the whole of its Providence lingers—the
Edge of the universe—
Who'd have thought,
so near,
A thin horizon line—
first and last exhale—
The edge of the universe—

my lips.
In one, the memory of *all*.

32

Details

Late at night, from afar, gently calling
  Standing there in the dark, a flood of white is still
  Trees by the tracks most presumably awakened
  Roaring whistle penetrates green veins, and following
  the tides as does the sea, drifts on until all shores are met

      Just the same as that irreplaceable split second
      when the sound of the engine shuts off, sweat rolls down neck,
      Face and arms smeared with dust and time
      Eyes burning through the heat, pounding life – true hard work;
      a driving reason

            Then, a similar coldness before the eves of subtle warmth,
            exists where the blue tint at dusk evolves and in the early
            morning trees the light runs about its track.
            A beaten hat rests on table, until it is called upon once again
            to define its *donner*

                  The repeating tune set forth by a mysterious
                  inhabitant of the skies--over and over it calls—
                  Like a sound of a reel, the line steadily draws in
                  the parallel waters come to from still sleep
                  The ringing of the birds and waters collide

Ingrid

Hers was a quiet sorrow.
She left before The Wall was built.
Four decades later she finds the years
have made a foreigner of her.
Her husband was mean. Her words. He is dead now.
No children will mourn her. She has none to speak of.
Schotzie died in her arms and then there was the German Shepherd.
He crawled away to his cave beneath her husband's desk,
closed his eyes, and left his pain behind
for Ingrid to discover.

Now we meet. I am driving the coach bus.
She is waiting for "the others" to return.
We visited Anderson's for lunch and the
nursery of flowers.
Ingrid is too tired to maintain a garden in
this humid climate.
The trees and songbirds hold her gaze—
her eyes are Alice blue, she is still on the surface—
but impatience finds voice and she is happy if the
others are done early and we can go.

She's lived someone else's life. She is attractive in
spite of age and a mean husband; she kept something
alive inside, but now it seems, she wonders—
what was it all for?

I don't ask if she is lonely.
It would be like asking a sea star
if it still feels the waves.

She'd have gone back all those years ago, right away if only—
it is not resignation I see nor bitterness. It is
subtle, charming in its sorrow—like a rose that continues to
bloom in spite of itself—she wears no thorns, but
instead bears her regret.

I start the engine and a lifetime condensed into half an hour
falls away.

I am glad she retired to the bus early.
Had she watched me walking into the sun?
It was a nice change, having someone to wait with—
someone who knows silence.
Profound sorrow allows no reply.
I hope she realized my silence was understanding.
I'm too young to hold her reflection in my face and yet—I do.
It took a long way to get here.
I'd have been good to you.

The Glade of Remembrance

Unto the glades of remembrance I descend.
The malaise of inertia impeded
disrobes by degrees.

How sharp the blades—cool
in their prickling betrayal of
all that was.

Awake, awake—rather a brooding
melancholy sweep me up and the
head of fore be furrowed in
gloomy delight than this
stuffy vessel chained below deck—
while life charges above, teeming
with purpose.
The ladder ascends, for I can
only climb, standing now
encased by the well of longing—
up, up, up.

The glade pricks my senses—
a restless impassioned spark—
kill the mundane—
I turn onto my ribs, inhale the
deep earth—let me sleep, let
me stay, let me dream—

Soon I shall fly away.

My Sister's Roses

PHILOMENE HOOD

Philomene was born in Houston, reared in the state of Kansas, received her M.A. in Modern Languages from the University of Kansas. She joins the Williamsburg Poetry Guild in their search for beauty in the perfect word. Her background in romance languages and her respect for Virginia's place in history lead to rich themes in her poetry. Her work features a lifetime of love for poetry, a generous and sincere emotion, and an enthusiasm for western lore and tradition. Three sons are a rich part of the living reality she expresses so well. Philomene delights in sharing poetically the experiences of her life.

A Bow to the Mystery

Bare-toed in sunshine,
I absently smoothed a landing strip
in the dust,
not expecting wind-borne freight,
not even hoping.

Two fluttering parcels,
unaware of welcome, came my way
obliquely,
on a breeze as light as breath.

A black velvet butterfly
edged with electric blue,
shining with life,
drifted gently to my runway—
no need for wings to wave
when a downdraft maps the flight.
It settled slowly,
acknowledged my toe.

A dry leaf, lifeless at last,
wearing brown fatigues,
swayed on a zephyr and came in
to a rendezvous.
It nudged the butterfly,
ignored my toe.

Ebony wings, antennae,
alive,
and a shy, dry leaf
came to companion me.
I hold them forever poised in sunshine,
and praise the mystery that composes such magic from
a breath of air.

Come Five O'Clock

Something happens when birthday cards
Suddenly appear again,
And friends we made just yesterday
Send cards that say "Remember when . . . ?"

Years have quietly slipped away
Leaving promissory notes,
"Paid," "Stay well!" and "Promise me . . . ."
Or memories enclosed in quotes.

It's time to phone a friend or two!
Set a table, or pour a drink,
Share a memory—or make one!
Better far to swim than sink.

Suddenly Twenty-five

Or maybe thirty
Throaty machines roared
Around the Mercedes,
(You know the kind—
Black leather jackets)
Wrestled low bushes,
Hustled red leaves skyward,
Trashed the sound barrier,
Left us shocked at the silence.

We paused at The Pub to recover.

Here they came!
Swerved in, scattering sand.
The rumble subsided.
Knights of the road—
Chest insignia,
Power and youth in charge of the world,
Goggles, masks,
Helmets gleaming like satin,
Polished boots studded with silver,
Worn smooth.

Oh, the girls! Satellites in jeans,
Designer jackets,
Their casual dismounts
A study in grace.
Slow removal of gloves,
Scarves unbound,
Saddle-bagged.
A tossing of hair, unbound.
High signs.

Suddenly twenty-five,
I fluffed my hair,
Swaggered, ever so slightly.

We rode home with the top down.

The Crest of the Mountain

The path leads gently upward, wide enough
To lend a moment's pause or offer choice—
To walk the safely smooth, or take the rough
And hear the siren's tantalizing voice.
A wind-blown creeper owns its rocky nook;
Views of forgotten valleys pierce the trail;
Unseen springs made marshes where deer took
Rest with the climber from the day's travail.
Far is the crest and far the welcome sight!
The staff, now needed, prods the stones away.
Lured on by eagles, spirit heir to flight,
The stumbling climber finds he cannot stray
The narrow path, the evening blush of sky,
The beckoning valley and the urge to fly.

Peaceful Island Marsh

JOANNE SCOTT KENNEDY

I gave myself "permission to write" after raising a large family and working as a reference librarian and book reviewer. A Christopher Wren class in memoir writing led to the four books of family history and stories that my husband Bob and I then put together as gifts for our children and grandchildren. When I later realized that some things can be said only in poetry, Rita Durrant's Christopher Wren class in poetry writing gave me not only skills but a mentor and friend. I like to slip beneath the skin of family secrets and happenings in my poetry, to write about the mysteries of memory, the interconnected beauties of our world, and the continuing bonds between the living and the dead.

43

The Gatekeeper

Do you remember, brother,
the pasture gate Grandpa creaked wide
on dewy mornings to lead Molly through,

bell clanging, left haunch, right...Mother
insisting one of us attend, each time, the stern
old German Pop she never spoke to...

we girls silent and scared as she when our
turns came, you (male and sure of welcome)
going with a smile.

Do you remember hanging on
the fence, long cornfields rustling green off
to the west, and to the east, the early freight

train pluming, whistling down the dawn
and far on past...up north, the sulfur creek
festooned both sides with elderberry bushes,

the rumble bridge the Snee boys' horses
pulled their wagon over, then up, up
to the farm we'd never seen inside the great
                              blue bowl of hills.

Gentle brother, three months ago
slow bells tolled you through the gate we'd long
pretended wasn't there—and you went unafraid.

I see you waiting, smiling, gate held
wide for sisters leaving fences, one by one.

Let's Go, Jo

The little airport restaurant
was so good it was crowded
                        every noon.

Finally Bob walked over,
assessed the situation, turned
and called out, strong voice warm,
                    "Let's go, Jo."

And why did all our fifty years
come welling up to burst in bloom
around my heart, flood every vein
                    with sudden joy?

        His voice, my name…

That Snake

I'm not entirely sure
      I've earned, or like, my status as pariah.
You've heard that suspect tale
    about some greedy woman and an apple,

I expect…but just watch this.
      A casual flex of muscle and my whole length
forms an S-shape as I glide—
      now isn't that a lovely motion?

And my colors;
      green as springtime grass, or rosy coral striped
with black; even dull brown rattlesnakes are diamonds,
      diamonds, from their flat heads

(lethal, I admit)
      down to those courteous rattles. Still—to see
horror rise in human eyes when I shift my head
      or flick my tongue or drape myself serenely

from a branch…I think I'd miss that if I were a soft-eyed
      doe relying on appeal, or a chipper, merely
pretty bluebird…

        Power is addictive, is it not?

White Springs

Out the old road on our bikes in chilly April,
a scraggly slope of pears in bloom, the gray day's

light caught in scanty white.   Silence on the hilltop...
shallow-water cellar hole and chimney-crumble,

a doorsill moldered into ghost, the narcissus clump
beside it overgrown and spotty white.

A woman
could have stepped across that sill into the smooth
swell of the evening—dishes done, babes bedded,

first push of sparkle through dark blue—looked down
the hill to watch tiered billows light themselves

to white, then to the clutch of white beside her feet—
swung between whites, intense fragrance coursing

through her.   She must have sorrowed
for the pear trees when the old truck turned the final

corner. She could have dug her white clump, wrapped
its root ball for the trip, or brushed the soil away

and bagged the bulbs. I wonder if she left it as sister
to the pears, so they could join the orphan scents

of April on the slope, beside the sill, swing a mother
moon between thinned whites.

Wrigley Field

RON LANDA

A Chicago-area native, Ron attended several universities, eventually earning a Ph.D. in American diplomatic history from Georgetown University in 1970. He briefly taught at College Misericordia and George Washington University. For thirty-nine years he served as a historian for the U.S. Department of State and for the Office of the Secretary of Defense, where he edited volumes in the documentary series, *Foreign Relations of the United States*, and co-authored *The McNamara Ascendancy, 1961–1965*. He began writing poetry in 2002. His collection of poems, *Drops in a Bucket*, was published in 2011. He enjoys ballroom and line dancing, golf, lawn bowling, travel, studying foreign languages, reading old-time mystery writers like Agatha Christie and Eric Ambler, and rooting for the Chicago Cubs. He and his wife Barb have three children and three grandchildren.

Carolina in the Morning

From the deck in light still gray, where the silly squirrels play,
    An' the dawn sneaks up like rabbits out o' bushes 'cross the way,
A piercing sound assaults me through the windows open wide,
    So shrill it's hard to like it--but, God knows, I've really tried.
The wee Carolina Wren, his trilling like measured screams,
    Makes certain I'll have no chance to revisit pleasant dreams.
I lie here thinking only of how to cut the chatter;
    The loss of precious shuteye is not a laughing matter.

        Go you back, you little birdie,
        As far as Winston-Salem.
        A noisier town than this,
        It's where you must have come from.

        Poetic justice there will be
        If you make this big mistake;
        For the students there all party late
        At the Forest known as Wake.

        Yes, rouse the sleeping students,
        And you'll surely get a shiner.
        Your blackened eye might look bad,
        But to me--
            Nothing could be finer.

Then as the days grow colder and the leaves begin to fall,
    The squirrels act more sober while a new bird comes to call.
From way up north they swoop down, the raucous Canada Geese,
    With their unholy honking, a bawling that does not cease.

        Go you back, you interlopers,
        All the way to Hudson Bay.
        Forget about Virginia;
        Here you'll never want to stay.

I suddenly remember all those noisy summer morns;
    How much sweeter they now seem than days ruined by goosy horns.
If only I could change this by saying a magic word
    And undo the wrong that I did when I banished that dear bird.

        Wren, Wren, Wren,
        You lovely, leather-lunged friend.
        Though I've cursed you and maligned you,
        By whate'er Power designed you,
        You're a better bird than they are,
        Carolina Wren!

The Case of Miss Marple's
Lost Marbles

Is it true Miss Marple's gone bonkers,
    that she quit St. Mary Mead
        and set out for Yonkers?

A sleuth on the looth, long in the tooth,
    she gave up knitting and went off aflitting,
looking there and here while mumbling, "Oh dear,"
    only to learn she had a fondness for beer.
She now lifts pretend barbells
    to strengthen "the little gray cells,"
straining for a *bon mot*
    to throw in the face of Poirot.

This all might be misdirection,
    what Christie works to perfection,
red herrings to lure us away
    from where truth really lay.
The marbles will no doubt turn up
    where everyone can see 'em--
in plain view next to Elgin's
    at the British Museum.

Crooks and Nannies
(With a Nod to the Reverend Spooner)

As farkness dell, Fiona and Rosie parked their prams
    outside a pavorite fub near Ciccadilly Pircus.
Over chish, fips, and plates full of pushy meas
    washed down with a pew fints and topped
by Badbury cars for dessert, they discussed
    how to skone their hills as thieves.
Already covered by scattle bars from lushes
    with the braw, they knew well the tisks
they would be raking. To the Tank bube station
    they trudged, searching for belephone tooths
and mending vachines to jiggle for choose lange
    before doing the higgest beist of their lives.
Alas, Constable Will Bhyte caught Rosie in the act
    of jiggling and slew her in the thrammer.
No wear-feather friend, Fiona visited Rosie often.
    "Can't you do something," Rosie asked,
"about the champ dill in here? The humbing and pleating
    system is terrible. And the bust dins are overflowing."
"Can't help there, dearie. But I'll get you out of here.
    It might be noisy, but it's lovely and sure to work.
        I'll bring you key and trumpets."

On the Edge
(Late December 2012)

As the year, not the world, comes to an end,
    perhaps silliness marks the start of a trend.
While the weather all 'round grows frightful,
    politicians act downright spiteful
as they rush toward a cliff,
    unsure whether it makes any diff.
There's general malaise in the milieu;
    people have lost patience to queue.
And no let-up in partisan polemic,
    though we're hit with a flu epidemic.
In doctors we no longer trust;
    after politicians they're the most cussed.
Shots they gave in September
    have no effect in December.
So we'll fill our coughers with pills,
    pay off overdue bills,
    then make a few changes in our wills.

Safe Harbor

EDWARD W. LULL

In his first career, Ed served in the U.S. Navy, primarily in submarines. After retiring in 1975, he began a second career as an executive in high-tech firms in the Washington, D.C. area. He later served as president and chairman of The Professional Group of Fairfax. In 1998, he began his writing career and joined the Poetry Society of Virginia (PSV). With PSV, he served four terms as president; he is a Life Member. His publications include: *Cabin Boy to Captain: A Sea Story; Where Giants Walked; The Sailors: Birth of a Navy; and Bits and Pieces: A Memoir.* For 10 years, he hosted a three-day poetry festival for PSV and has organized monthly poetry readings in Williamsburg since 2001. He is chairman of the Emerson Society of Williamsburg and a member of the Christopher Newport University Writers Council. He was the 2012 recipient of the Emyl Jenkins Award "for inspiring a love of writing and writing education in Virginia." Ed earned his B.S. at the U.S. Naval Academy and M.S. at George Washington University.

Evolution of Opinion

1960

My brother and I boarded the plane,
a business trip to San Diego
we had eagerly anticipated.
Our pilot welcomed us
with a smooth, standard spiel.
"Do you see how old that geezer is?
I hope he doesn't have a heart attack
before we get to San Diego."
Yeah, I wonder when the airline
retires these guys. Did you notice
that woman that boarded ahead of us?
She must be 60, struggling to look 40.
"Why do they do that?"

2010

A long-awaited fishing adventure,
a Christmas present from our wives,
put Bob and me on a plane to Florida.
After a brief welcome by the pilot, Bob said:
"I can't believe how these airlines
entrust the responsibility of the lives
of all these passengers to youngsters.
Where's the experience?"
Yeah, I'd feel much more comfortable
if I saw some gray hair.
How about that woman across the aisle;
she must be about 60.
"Man, she's hot!"

Ghost Fleet

As seagulls follow in our V-shaped wake
and sun rays make the ripples seem in flames,
we cruise beneath clear skies, an ideal day,
for boating down the broad, historic James.

Dense foliage, emerald-hued, lines both the shores
providing nature's border for the scene.
But moving east, the landscape's beauty melts,
and man-made structures soon replace the green.

To port, an unexpected sight appears:
large hulls topped by a forest of ships' masts.
Old merchantmen recline in silent prayer,
where condemnation hides their glorious pasts.

They carried worldly goods on seven seas,
and braved the fiercest storms and highest waves.
Appeals all spent, now they are forced to wait
like death row inmates, focused on their graves.

They know it's not their final resting place;
they're in their Purgatory here on earth.
Accepting fate is hard for those once proud,
acknowledging that now they have no worth.

Our boat turns 'round and we head back upstream,
the verdant landscape visible again.
My mind retains the vision of the ships
where age, neglect, and rust are their domain.

I wondered if one day it might be judged
that my productive, useful days were done.
Would I be anchored somewhere like those ships,
just pleased to feel the warmth of mid-day sun?

Green Mountain Magic

Our auto bumps along the gravel road;
a picnic on Mount Equinox we planned.
The engine whimpers at the climbing load,
but on we push till deep in timberland.

Continuing on foot we find a glade,
an overlook where we can see for miles.
The azure sky offsets the forest jade;
serenity of summertime beguiles.

A blanket spread for comfort, picnic starts,
we feel we are alone in Nature's world.
This setting is idyllic for sweethearts;
but caution flags refuse to be unfurled.

Enchantment of the moment overcomes
restraints and inhibitions of our youth.
The passion of the picnic soon succumbs
to promises encased in love and truth.

Some three decades have passed as now we drive
the well-paved highway to the parking spot.
The climb, a challenge now, but we arrive;
the clearing is still here, but changed somewhat.

A fuzzy haze diminishes our view;
the sky less blue, the pines and oaks less green.
But nonetheless our picnic would ensue;
though things had changed, this site remains serene.

Commitment to this day made years ago
drew us to Equinox this summer day.
Were hidden reasons there? We didn't know.
We spread the fruit and cheese and Chardonnay.

I look at her, my hands begin to shake;
I recognize we've entered love's domain.
At once the sleeping passions come awake;
our mountain works its magic once again.

The Hurdler
(A Lento)

Before race day arrived, she always would
explore the type of hurdles and the track.
Therefore, when on the line her focus could
ignore all things that might just hold her back.

Today, her competition would be great;
"Display your confidence," her coach had said.
"Replay in mind your fastest race to date;
 portray the winner; you'll end up ahead!"

      *   *   *   *   *   *   *   *

Beside the finish line were telltale clocks;
clear-eyed she saw the zeroes thereupon.
Trackside she slowly headed toward her blocks;
"Decide your strategy," she told herself.

Gun in his hand, the starter said aloud,
"Run in your lanes. Now hurdlers take your marks."
Fun time is over. "Set!" This hushed the crowd.
Sun in her eyes, she startles from her dream.

Minneapolis at Twilight

LOUISE SHARER

Louise was born in Minneapolis and lived in the same house her great-great-grandfather built on the banks of the Mississippi in 1862. She is married to William, a physician, and has three children: Kate, Molly, and David. Armed with a B.A. in journalism and an M.B.A., Louise embarked upon a rewarding career in corporate marketing where writing played an essential role. After retiring as a senior vice president from a global financial firm, she and her husband moved to Williamsburg. Throughout her career she found writing prose and poetry a welcome escape from the demands of corporate life.

Afghani Mother

A lifeless child stiffens in her arms.
Yesterday now vague and distant,
viewed through lenses
dulled by cataracts of war.
Tomorrow's meaning lost.
Reason knocks on a bolted door.
She swaddles him in emotional gauze.
A precious gift sacrificed to hate.
The god of evil offers no gratitude,
it only stares back, blank and cold.
Like the eyes of her lifeless child.

Shared Parting

In silence we walk
not as lovers, but once loved.
Hand-in-hand, one final time.
Entwined fingers belie our fraying,
like cable coiled and worn
on the deck of an abandoned ship.
Weathered rope no longer tethers,
words unspoken speak.
Indifference now where worship was,
splintered fibers moor no more.

The Street I Call Home

The parade is too long.
The bands march.
I hear no melody.
No drums,
trumpets,
cymbals.
Silent soldiers.
Floats pass.
Blurred, muted color.
Shapeless.
Coagulated textures.
I stare,
but do not see.
Tiaras glisten
in scorching sun.
Princesses wave
from convertible cars.
Their motions slowed.
They look deranged
Or is it I?
Stop.
This ceaseless series
of sequenced charades.
Go home.
Please.
Return my street
to me.

Twilight in the City

Night's leading lady
emerges silently
upon her stage.
Headlights twinkle
with anticipation,
jewels within her crown.
Mirrored windows
reflect her image,
shadows give it up.
Her pale hand
pulls daylight's shade,
a filmy hue.
She performs
her presence felt,
quiets city din.
Daytime tempos yield
to evening rhythms,
a dance on tipped toes.
With final bow
she steps aside,
until tomorrow's cue.

The Garden at St. Bede's

JOYCE CARR STEDELBAUER

HAVE YOU MET EVE?
HAVE YOU SEEN THE STAR?
WHO ROLLED THE STONE?
WHERE ARE YOU, ADAM?

This inspirational speaker asks thought provoking questions inviting her audience to share in the meditations. She and her husband, George, worship at Williamsburg Community Chapel. She has written an extensive collection of travel poetry her friends are urging her to publish. Even so, perhaps the next book will be titled:

OH, MAASAI BABY, WILL YOU STILL WEAR STRIPED STOCKINGS WHEN YOU TAKE THE BUS TO TOWN?

AFTERMATH

ADDITION

9/11/01 scenes scorch the walls near the ticket booth.
Flames leap to the ceiling and sear the soul.
Why here?
Why this jarring juxtaposition of attack and accident
on a dingy side street in Kiev, Ukraine?
The addition of 9/11 to 4/86 is strange math indeed.
Continue adding 76 villages, 90 K, 30 years
adding loss and distance and time to thousands of lives.
An incalculable sum total of grief, red as rosy apples
spinning down the museum staircase from painted trees,
branches angled in tortured anguish.

SUBTRACTION

Under a great bird crafted of netting, wings of black
and white spread wide in flight like doves of peace
fleeing from ravenous vultures hungry for blood.
We sink to small stools before a video screen---
a helicopter speaker blaring orders to evacuate
almost drowned out by the screams of terrified children
being bundled into buses to be hurried away for "2-3 days."
In the center stands an altar from a local church
surrounded by the hauntingly beautiful young faces
subtracted from life.

MULTIPLICATION

Multiply disasters of radiated fields, infected fish thrashing
the waterways flowing south to Kiev, the populous capital.
Include the silenced factories and skeleton stores
idling in ghost towns dancing a macabre circle of death
times the loss of 76 villages and corrupted fields condemned
for 30 years. Count the cost of babies born with deformities
and cancers riding the winds across frozen fields.

DIVISION

Divide the guilt of accident or unauthorized experiment--
Ukrainian workers or Russian authorities---admission of explosion
or cover-up--immediate evacuation or wait and see---
calling for expert disaster help or "let the people celebrate May Day,"
with dances and contaminated flowers.
Divide lies from truth---76 village signs, traditional black
and white slashed with red meaning Finished.
Overhead a wreath of indigenous wormwood---translation Chernobyl,
as noted in the *New York Times,* can it be divided from Revelation 8:15

Remembering Rembrandt

The light lingers long
after the silver sun enfolds the green walls.
A serving girl snuffs the last lamp, yet,
reluctant to bed, stands in the shadows
longing to understand the scene,
forever caught eavesdropping.

The mother leans on the doorframe,
weakened in waiting, the costly currency
of her tears all spent in prayer.

A gentleman neighbor sinks to the step,
legs crossed, arm folded, dressed in disbelief,
his black hat weighted with wonder
as he studies the kneeling figure.

But the brother, the elder brother stands
richly robed, straight as pride.
Hands clasped in judgment on his walking staff,
beard carefully trimmed, and important turban
accentuates the height of his critical spirit.
No welcome in his eyes.
The Cimmerian night shrouds all questions.

But the light lingers long,
the eternal glow of the Father's face
bathes the errant son, no longer lost
like a wayward sheep or a widow's coin,
but found.
Healing hands embrace the son
with unconditional love,
his scabby, wretched form pressed close
to the Father's heart.

No questions. No judgment. No price of repatriation.
The blood-red robe spreads wide.
A mantle for the miscreant,
the miserable,
the misused.

The Prodigal is home.

A Spanish Shawl

This morning's skies are knitted of silvery-blue
eyelash yarn purled with threads of gold.
The reluctant spring flirts from behind
her pleated fan---a flash of pink and white almond
blossoms dance across the undulating land.

Cherimoyas ripen slowly into luscious green globes
patterned with a sculptor's fingertips.
I spoon the soft, sweet flesh with seeds
as big as Spanish eyes and watch the fading moon.

The winter jasmine flounces her feathery skirts
intoxicating April air with mysterious perfume.
Oranges linger long, rivaling nascent blossoms
on their bending boughs.

The sturdy figs are shy of green,
timid to swell their gift too soon.
Mediterranean vegetables cling to leafy beds
but generous geraniums nod their rosy heads.

The gallant sun strides across the mountains
earlier every day while March winds
sweep lingering clouds away.
The tented blue will stretch from
Gibraltar's Pillars to Haifa's heights.

The doves coo from the garden wall
and seem not to notice anything at all.
Lovers cuddle close at midnight
like the sea to the sleeping shore
and know that all will be as it has been before.

ALEGRIA

The Altar of the Basilica of St. Bede

The Altar stands alone
atop a platform, round as planet Earth
supported by the very breath of God.
Three stone stairs trace the circumference,
both barrier and gate to all
who would presume to enter here.
The brilliant block, wrestled from the womb of time,
metamorphosed by ancient fire deep in the Carrara.
Of such marble, Michelangelo sculpted young King David
and passionate pietas of Mary the Virgin
with the promised Messiah.

The Altar stands alone,
white-cloud marble chiseled now to a perfect square.
Under workmen's careful hands, sixteen side carvings
suggest pillars shouldering mighty weight:
perhaps the twelve tribes of our foundation
or twelve apostles of faith fused like limestone
into marble truth of the four gospels.
Cold as the melting snows of Mt. Hermon
rushing to freshen the Sea of Galilee,
sparse gray veins run like the Jordan River
and the Jabbok stream into the Dead Sea,
prophesied to flow fresh and sweet when Messiah reigns.

The Altar stands alone -
open, accessible to all repentant people
desiring confirmation of forgiveness;
reminiscent of altars of sacrifice in the wilderness,
altars of thanksgiving in the Beautiful Land.
To commune with the Living God,
partake of the Bread of His Presence
and the costly Cup of His Salvation;
love lavished on a lonely world
by the Resurrected Messiah.

*"Come all ye who are heavy laden
and I will give you rest."*

San Juan Valley

ELIZABETH J. URQUHART

Elizabeth was born in Greeley, Colorado and grew up on the edge of the Navajo reservation in the San Juan Valley in New Mexico. Many of her poems are written about the people of the Southwest. She began writing in the third grade and two years later was awarded first place in the county competition for her story about a goat.

She earned a B.A. degree in English Literature and History from the University of Iowa and an M.A. in Reading Education from Old Dominion University in Norfolk. For nineteen years she taught reading in the Hampton, Virginia schools. She is grateful for the support of the Williamsburg Poetry Guild and the Live Wire Press where her poems have been published for the last ten years.

Her three children grown and scattered, she lives with her Irish husband and five cats in Hampton.

La Bruja

Baby Doll, dark eyes, happy smile, is jean-clad.
He's interested in the people, in his father's bar,
and is a favorite of La Bruja,
that Andalusian Lady from gypsy stock--
Tall and lanky, stringy hair, sharp eyes,
she throws salt over the shoulder
and makes a cross on the floor before dancing.
She's fond of the boy and calls him "Baby Doll".
The feathered owl perched on a limb,
hoots and laughs, but is shot under the wing
by the rancher who knows it's a witch.
Baby Doll later sees the wound under La Bruja's arm.
This Bruja, who casts good spells and bad spells, is gone,
but remembered by her Baby Doll.

Lost Boy

I look in the mirror and see
high aquiline cheeks sharply edged,
dark eyes, and a face the color of earth,
the face of a young Navajo man.

When I was three, small, runny nosed, crying loudly,
I was taken by white people to a mission school.
My brothers and sisters and the parents who adopted me are not part of me.
I am neither white nor Indian. Where do I belong?
The healing ceremonies and customs of my tribe are foreign to me.

I've wandered through my life's journey with faltering footsteps.
When I look at jagged red bluffs and cerulean skies, I think,
"Is Mother Earth mine?
Is she close to the white man's God?
Where are the spirits of my ancestors?"

On a warm, yellow-red fall day, I return to Monument Valley,
the home of my family, my Navajo family.
The cousins, sister, and Aunt Hodezbah enclose me in their arms.
They cry, in Navajo, "He has returned to us. He has grown into a man."
Heavy silver turquoise bracelets brush my forehead.
My Aunt Hodezbah, with tears running down her cheeks, says,
"He has been away, far from us.
We, who love him, will teach him and keep him here."

Preacher Lewis

Preacher Lewis was an Episcopal priest,
small and wiry, gingery hair
which stuck straight up most of the time.
Short, pointed ears and a generous mouth,
given to hearty bellows of laughter
when he wasn't proclaiming the Word.
His eyes, bright blue, penetrated one's very being,
bits of whiskers dotted his unshaven jaw.
Dressed in worn jeans,
with a white collar around his knobbledy neck,
he rode the Denver and Rio Grande Western
(the old steam train) up and down its tracks.
He baptized the conductor, the engineer, the fireman,
porters, and any baby who happened to be riding along.
All babies received a baby cap knitted by Preacher himself.

Preacher, the bane of the Bishop's existence,
lived a free and happy life.
His was a life dedicated completely to the Lord,
who, he knew, understood his every move.
A frequent visitor to the bars and saloons,
he refused all alcoholic beverages
but passed around his old moth-eaten hat.
"Boys," he said to the card-playing cowhands,
*"Fill up the hat with money, paper money to feed
and clothe Widow Brown's children."*
"The Preacher is here," they all said putting down their drinks
and cards, *"Listen to the Preacher."*
"Boys," Preacher said,
"Lift up your eyes unto the Lord for you are truly blessed."

River Stones

I dream of river stones
worn smooth by the quiet waters of the San Juan.
I dream of river stones cemented together to form a building.
A two-story building with a cross on top.
A hospital for the Dineh--the people,
perched upon a hill above the glistening, gliding river.
The building has wards for sick Navajo and a jewel of a chapel,
with an altar covered with petrified wood and bits of Anasazi pottery.
A sheepskin soft, white as a creamy quilt, covers the steps,
Navajo rugs, red, black, grey and white lie upon the sanctuary floor.
I see my father in his vestments, green for Advent,
celebrating Mass.
Later, my elfin mother pumps the pedals of the organ
and we lustily sing our favorite hymns.
I hear my sister and me, giggling,
as Jim Begay, large black hat by his side,
sticks his gum behind his left ear.
He is our true love; we delight in his antics.
I dream of river stones worn smooth by the water,
but memories remain sharp and colorful in the mind.

Laughing Gulls

E. S. VON GEHREN

Raised in that part of New Jersey known as the North Jersey Shore, I grew up along the banks of the Navesink River, spending my days exploring life at the water's edge. The river served as my first teacher, instilling in me a love of exploration and curiosity for all things of nature and science. I intended to become an astrophysicist but found the realm of the human mind to be as vast and unfathomable, so I switched goals and got my degrees in experimental psychology.

My career spanned both Federal Government and the private sector in Human Factors research, and included working with the ARPAnet (precursor to the Internet). Yet I have always had a passion for the many art forms and vehicles we use to express human emotion: music, sculpture, painting, and language. I had thought that upon retiring I would once again take up painting, but no, it is my poetry that once again stirs my blood and shapes my world. It is the taste and textures of words, in their most synesthetic exuberance, that urge me to capture the rhythms of my inner life on paper. Though it is music that fills my soul, it is words that fill my life and thoughts. I shall exist as long as my words are here for you to read.

Stars

One-eyed creatures peering
Through black cloth
Of night sky.

Twinkling! Blinkling! Winkling!
Or have they a steady gaze
Shifted by currents of warm summer air?

Are they just out of reach
Of strong-armed archer's shaft;
Or, perhaps, countless distances
Too great to understand
By earthly experience?

Mystery to the Ancients.
Still a mystery
To those who dig
Deeply into the fire
Of their origin.

The reality of cold scientific fact
Overtakes the pleasure prompted
By their mystery,
The titillation of our imagination.

I am caught in both worlds.
The science is understandable
And comforting,
But oh how I love the drama
Of the imagined.

Beguiled by the Beat

Rubbing elbows it's called.
Just take care not to spill your drink,
or another's on you.
Idle blather surrounds me, blah,
blah, blah.

Then I see her across the room, talking.
She looks in my direction …
smiles.
My heart flutters,
flutters, flutters.

Am I so easily beguiled?
I don't even know her.
Yet the noise of the room is masked
as blood in my ears pulses,
pulses, pulses.

She leaves her group and crosses towards me.
I watch the sheen of her dress slide
across her thigh with each stride.
Her steps bringing her closer,
closer, closer.

Extending her hand she caresses mine.
Her scent intoxicates me as she breathes,
"I have so wanted to meet you."
I lose all sense of place, caught in the moment
moment, moment.

I am overtaken with passion.
I lean close so others will not hear.
"I love you."
I repeat it over,
over, over.

She straightens up and introduces herself.
"Excuse me, but I am the wife of your host."
I cringe.
I am a fool,
fool, fool.

Perhaps It Was a Little Girl

Who made the silly pig nose
that marked the outside door?
Who left the messy crumb trail
of cookies on the floor?
You say, "It was the neighbor's dog;
it's something puppies do."
Perhaps it was a little girl
who looks a lot like you.

Who made the silly faces
at the mirror in the hall?
Who left the dirty handprints
and the smudges on the wall?
You say, "It was the neighbor's kid;
it's something children do."
Perhaps it was a little girl
who looks a lot like you.

Who snuggles close, all sleepy,
upon her mommy's lap?
Who gives big hugs and kisses
when taken for her nap?
You say, "It is the neighbor's cat;
it's something kittens do."
But, I think it is a little girl
who looks just like you.

Laughing Gull

Follower of boat
Rider of breeze
Catcher of bread
You, Black-headed
Laughing Gull

Long tapered wings
Master of sea air gusts
You dip and turn with ease
In pursuit of food and frolic

Only at rest when sitting
On pile at dock-side
With others not your kind
None so handsome as you

Though they preen and try
None is able to match
Body suited in grey and white
Head of deepest-black
Laughing Gull

A song like no other
Though not the lyric kind
Part chortle, rasp, shout
Hints of hidden pleasure

Is life so amusing
Or is your mirth but a taunt
Mocking with haughty voice
Kin and stranger alike

Perhaps the joke is on us
Obeying your demand with bread
No, humor is a kinder thought
That is why we call you
Laughing Gull

CREDITS

Cover: *Wisteria*: Wheston Chancellor Grove

Flora Bolling Adams and Friend: Ann Marie Boyden

Sunrise: Ann Marie Boyden

Dogwoods: Ann Marie Boyden

Little Cottonwood Canyon: Ann Marie Boyden

Emily Dickinson Museum: Ann Marie Boyden

House above the Sea: Ann Marie Boyden

The Backyard: Wheston Chancellor Grove

Windlust: Wheston Chancellor Grove

My Sister's Roses: Ann Marie Boyden

Peaceful Island Marsh: Ann Marie Boyden

Wrigley Field: Steve Dorer/Shutterstock.com

Safe Harbor: Wheston Chancellor Grove

Minneapolis at Twilight: Pete Spiro/Shutterstock.com

The Garden at St. Bede's: Wheston Chancellor Grove

San Juan Valley: Jeffery M. Frank/Shutterstock.com

Laughing Gulls: Ann Marie Boyden

The Williamsburg Poetry Guild: Dr. J. I. A.Urquhart

Quill Illustration: khandisha/Shutterstock.com

Design: Kenric Graphics, Inc.

The Williamsburg Poetry Guild

Front row left to right: Flora Bolling Adams, Rita Durrant, Philomene Hood, Elizabeth J. Urquhart. *Back row, left to right:* Ron Landa, Joanne Goode, Joanne Scott Kennedy, Joyce Carr Stedelbauer, Dianne Jordan, E. S. von Gehren, Wheston Chancellor Grove, Ann Marie Boyden. *Not pictured:* Louise Sharer, Edward W. Lull.